Scott Foresman
SCIENCE

Lab Manual

Grade 5

Scott Foresman 5

Scott Foresman

Editorial Offices: Glenview, Illinois; Parsippany, New Jersey; New York, New York
Sales Offices: Reading, Massachusetts; Duluth, Georgia; Glenview, Illinois
Carrollton, Texas; Ontario, California

www.sfscience.com

Contributors

Series Authors

Dr. Timothy Cooney
*Professor of Earth Science and
    Science Education*
Earth Science Department
University of Northern Iowa
Cedar Falls, Iowa

Michael Anthony Dispezio
Science Education Specialist
Cape Cod Children's Museum
Falmouth, Massachusetts

Barbara K. Foots
Science Education Consultant
Houston, Texas

Dr. Angie L. Matamoros
Science Curriculum Specialist
Broward County Schools
Ft. Lauderdale, Florida

Kate Boehm Nyquist
Science Writer and Curriculum Specialist
Mount Pleasant, South Carolina

Dr. Karen L. Ostlund
Professor
Science Education Center
The University of Texas at Austin
Austin, Texas

Contributing Authors

Dr. Anna Uhl Chamot
*Associate Professor and
ESL Faculty Advisor*
Department of Teacher Preparation
    and Special Education
Graduate School of Education
    and Human Development
The George Washington University
Washington, D.C.

Dr. Jim Cummins
Professor
Modern Language Centre and
    Curriculum Department
Ontario Institute for Studies in Education
Toronto, Canada

Gale Phillips Kahn
Lecturer, Science and Math Education
Elementary Education Department
California State University, Fullerton
Fullerton, California

Vince Sipkovich
Teacher
Irvine United School District
Irvine, California

Steve Weinberg
Science Consultant
Connecticut State Department
    of Education
Hartford, Connecticut

ISBN 0-673-59342-8

Copyright © 2000, Addison-Wesley Educational Publishers, Inc.

All rights reserved. The blackline masters in this publication are designed to be used with appropriate equipment to reproduce copies for classroom use only. Scott Foresman grants permission to classroom teachers to reproduce these masters.

Printed in the United States of America

7890 PO 03 02

Safety in Science

Scientists know they must work safely when doing experiments. You need to be careful when doing experiments too. These are some safety tips to remember.

Safety Tips

- Read each experiment carefully.
- Wear cover goggles when needed.
- Clean up spills right away.
- Never taste or smell substances unless directed to do so by your teacher.
- Handle sharp items carefully.
- Tape sharp edges of materials.
- Handle thermometers carefully.
- Use chemicals carefully.
- Dispose of chemicals properly.
- Put materials away when you finish an experiment.
- Wash your hands after each experiment.

© Scott Foresman 5

Science Inquiry

Throughout your science classes, you will ask questions, do investigations, answer your questions, and tell others what you have learned. Use the descriptions below to help you during your scientific inquiries.

How fast will an ice cube melt at different temperatures?

1 Ask questions that can be answered by scientific investigations.

Direct your questions and inquiries toward objects and events that can be described, explained, or predicted by scientific investigations.

2 Design and conduct a scientific investigation.

Investigations can include using scientific methods to carry out science inquiry. As you conduct your investigations, you will relate your ideas to current scientific knowledge, suggest alternate explanations, and evaluate explanations and procedures.

3 Use appropriate tools and methods to gather, analyze, and interpret data.

The tools and methods you use will depend on the questions you ask and the investigations you design. A computer can be a useful tool for collecting, summarizing, and displaying your data.

4 Use data to develop descriptions, suggest explanations, make predictions, and construct models.

Base your explanations and descriptions on the information that you have gathered. In addition, understanding scientific subject matter will help you develop explanations, identify causes, and recognize relationships of events you observe with science content.

5 Use logic to make relationships between data and explanations.

Review and summarize the data you have gathered in your investigation. Use logic to determine the cause and effect relationships in the events and variables you observe.

6 Analyze alternative explanations and predictions.

Listen to, consider, and evaluate explanations offered by others. Asking questions and querying and evaluating explanations are part of scientific inquiry.

7 Communicate procedures and explanations.

Share your investigations with others by describing your methods, observations, results, and explanations.

8 Use mathematics to analyze data and construct explanations.

Use mathematics in your investigations to gather, organize, and collect data and to present explanations and results in a meaningful manner.

© Scott Foresman 5

Using Scientific Methods for Science Inquiry

Scientists try to solve many problems. Scientists study problems in different ways, but they all use scientific methods to guide their work. Scientific methods are organized ways of finding answers and solving problems. Scientific methods include the steps shown on these pages. The order of the steps or the number of steps used may change. You can use these steps to organize your own scientific inquiries.

Which gets hot faster, water or sand?

State the Problem

The problem is the question you want to answer. Curiosity and inquiry have resulted in many scientific discoveries. State your problem in the form of a question.

Formulate Your Hypothesis

Your hypothesis is a possible answer to your problem. Make sure your hypothesis can be tested. Your hypothesis should take the form of a statement.

▲ *Sand heats up faster than water.*

Fill one pie pan with water and another with sand. Put a thermometer in each pan. Let them stand until they reach the same temperature.▼

Identify and Control the Variables

For a fair test, you must select which variable to change and which variables to control. Choose one variable to change when you test your hypothesis. Control the other variables so they do not change.

© Scott Foresman 5

Test Your Hypothesis

Do experiments to test your hypothesis. You may need to repeat experiments to make sure your results remain consistent. Sometimes you conduct a scientific survey to test a hypothesis.

▲ *Direct a heat source on each pan.*

Collect Your Data

As you test your hypothesis, you will collect data about the problem you want to solve. You may need to record measurements. You might make drawings or diagrams. Or you may write lists or descriptions. Collect as much data as you can while testing your hypothesis.

Temperature of Water and Sand						
Time (minutes)	0	1	2	3	4	5
Water	22°					
Sand	22°					

Interpret Your Data

By organizing your data into charts, tables, diagrams, and graphs, you may see patterns in the data. Then you can decide what the information from your data means.

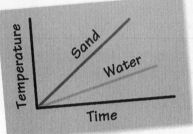

State Your Conclusion

Your conclusion is a decision you make based on evidence. Compare your results with your hypothesis. Based on whether or not your data supports your hypothesis, decide if your hypothesis is correct or incorrect. Then communicate your conclusion by stating or presenting your decision.

Sand heats faster than water.

Inquire Further

Use what you learn to solve other problems or to answer other questions that you might have. You may decide to repeat your experiment, or to change it based on what you learned.

▼ *Which cools faster, water or sand?*

© Scott Foresman 5

Using Process Skills for Science Inquiry

These 12 process skills are used by scientists when they do their research. You also use many of these skills every day. For example, when you think of a statement that you can test, you are using process skills. When you gather data to make a chart or graph, you are using process skills. As you do the activities in your lab manual, you will use these same process skills.

Observing

Use one or more of your senses— seeing, hearing, smelling, touching, or tasting—to gather information about objects or events.

▲ *Tools can help in making observations*

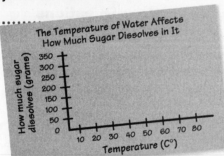

Communicating

Share information about what you learn using words, pictures, charts, graphs, and diagrams.

Classifying

Arrange or group objects according to their common properties.

▲ *Objects that are attracted to a magnet.*

Objects that are not attracted to a magnet. ▼

An apple's mass is about 150 grams. Its diameter is 6.5 centimeters. ▼

Estimating and Measuring

Make an estimate about an object's properties, then measure and describe the object in units.

Inferring

Draw a conclusion or make a reasonable guess based on what you observe, or from your past experiences.

I can infer that increasing the thickness of the paper or plastic decreases the effect of the magnetic force.

© Scott Foresman 5

Predicting

Form an idea about what will happen based on evidence.

▲ *Predict how five sheets of paper would affect the magnetic force.*

A mold is an impression made by an object in a substance... . ▼

Making Operational Definitions

Define or describe an object or event based on your experiences with it.

Making and Using Models

Make real or mental representations to explain ideas, objects, or events.

▲ *The model is different from a molecule because... . It's like a molecule because... .*

If you plant a seed upside down, the root will grow toward.... ▼

Formulating Questions and Hypotheses

Think of a statement that you can test to solve a problem or to answer a question about how something works.

Collecting and Interpreting Data

Gather observations and measurements into graphs, tables, charts, or diagrams. Then use the information to solve problems or answer questions.

Water evaporated faster in warm air than in cold air.

Variables	
Change	Same
✓ Temperature of water	✓ Kind of fish
	✓ Size and shape of bowl
	✓ Amount of water in bowl
	✓ Light
	✓ Food

Identifying and Controlling Variables

Change one factor that may affect the outcome of an event while holding other factors constant.

Experimenting

Design an investigation to test a hypothesis or to solve a problem. Then form a conclusion.

I'll plan an experiment and use scientific methods to test my hypothesis.

Contents
Part 1: Activity Record Sheets

© Scott Foresman 5

© Scott Foresman 5

Name _____ Date _____

Exploring Life Characteristics

Explore

3. Record your **observations** of the contents of the bottles and of the balloons.

_____

_____

_____

_____

_____

_____

_____

_____

_____

Reflect

1. Make an **inference** to answer the following question: Which shows signs of life, the yeast or the sand? Explain.

_____

_____

_____

_____

_____

_____

_____

_____

© Scott Foresman 5

2. What signs of life did you observe in this activity?

_____

_____

_____

_____

_____

_____

Inquire Further

What would happen to the yeast cells if you did not add sugar to the water? Develop a plan to answer this or other questions you may have.

_____

_____

_____

_____

_____

Self-Assessment Checklist	
I followed instructions to **observe** a mixture of yeast, sugar, and water.	_____
I followed instructions to **observe** a mixture of sand, sugar, and water.	_____
I recorded my observations of the contents of the bottle and the balloons.	_____
I made **inferences** about whether sand or yeast was living.	_____
I listed the signs of life I observed.	

 Notes for Home Your child explored what happens when yeast and sugar are mixed together.
Home Activity: With your child, look at the ingredients in a yeast bread recipe and discuss what causes the bread to rise.

© Scott Foresman 5

Observing Growth of Fungi

Follow This Procedure

4. Record your observations in the chart.

Mold observations			
Day	**Bread**	**Orange peel**	**Tomato**
1			
2			
3			
4			
5			
6			
7			

Interpret Your Results

1. Compare and contrast the mold growth on the different foods. Does the same kind of mold grow on different types of food? Does mold spread from one piece of food to the one next to it? Did any piece of food have more than one kind of mold on it?

_____

_____

_____

_____

_____

_____

_____

© Scott Foresman 5

3. Make an **inference** based on your data and observations to explain how you think molds get energy. Why do you think mold can grow in the dark?

_____

_____

_____

_____

Inquire Further

Could the molds grow without water? in a sunny spot? Develop a plan to answer these or other questions you may have.

_____

_____

_____

_____

Self-Assessment Checklist	
I followed instructions to **observe** mold growth on different foods.	_____
I **collected data** by recording my observations of mold growth.	_____
I **interpreted data** by comparing and contrasting mold growth on different foods.	_____
I **communicated** by comparing and contrasting my results with the results of other students.	_____
I made **inferences** about how molds get energy and why mold can grow in the dark.	_____

 Notes for Home Your child **observed** the growth of fungi.
Home Activity: Explain to your child that mold grows on the north side of trees and ask your child to speculate why.

© Scott Foresman 5

Exploring Cells

Explore

4–5. Record your observations in the chart.

	Drawing of observations
Onion	
Elodea	

Reflect

1. Compare and contrast the cells of the onion and elodea plant.

_____

_____

_____

_____

_____

_____

© Scott Foresman 5

2. Make an **inference.** What other things might cells do for the plant besides making food?

_____

_____

_____

_____

Inquire Further

What do other cells look like? Develop a plan to answer this or other questions you may have.

_____

_____

_____

_____

_____

_____

_____

Self-Assessment Checklist	
I followed instructions to **observe** the cells of an onion.	_____
I followed instructions to **observe** the cells of an elodea plant.	_____
I made drawings of my observations.	_____
I compared and contrasted the onion and elodea cells.	_____
I made an **inference** about plant cells.	_____

Notes for Home Your child **observed** onion skin cells and elodea cells.
Home Activity: With your child, look at pictures of cells from other plants or animals and compare and contrast them to the cells from the onion and elodea.

© Scott Foresman 5

Name _____ Date _____

Investigating the Life Cycle of a Flowering Plant

Follow This Procedure

3–4. Record your data and observations in the chart.

Date	Observations	Plant height	Drawing of plant

Interpret Your Results

1. Describe how the plant developed from the time you began to observe it until seeds were formed?

_____

_____

_____

_____

_____

_____

_____

© Scott Foresman 5

2. Predict what would happen if you planted your seeds.

_____

_____

_____

_____

_____

_____

_____

Inquire Further

Would the plant grow faster if you changed how much water or fertilizer you gave it? Develop a plan to answer this or other questions you may have.

_____

_____

_____

_____

_____

Self-Assessment Checklist	
I followed directions to grow and pollinate a radish plant.	_____
I recorded my **observations.**	_____
I **measured** the height of the plant.	_____
I **collected** and **interpreted data** and described the plant's development.	_____
I **predicted** what would happen to the new seeds if I planted them.	_____

Notes for Home Your child **observed** the stages in the life cycle of a flowering plant by growing and pollinating a radish plant.
Home Activity: Call a local nursery to find out what kind of fertilizer different plants need and why.

© Scott Foresman 5

Name _____   Date _____

Investigating Dominant and Recessive Traits

Follow This Procedure

6–9. Record your observations in the chart.

Parents	Offspring		
	RR (red)	Rr (red)	rr (white)
RR x Rr			
Total			
Rr x Rr			
Total			

Interpret Your Results

1. How many red-flowered offspring and how many white-flowered offspring are produced when one parent has two genes for red flowers and one parent is hybrid?

_____

_____

_____

_____

_____

© Scott Foresman 5

2. How many red-flowered offspring and how many white-flowered offspring are produced when both parents are hybrid?

_____

_____

_____

3. What can you **infer** from your data about inheritance of dominant and recessive traits?

_____

_____

_____

Inquire Further

How would your results be different if you tossed a chip for a hybrid (Rr) and a chip for two recessive genes (rr)? Develop a plan to answer this or other questions you may have.

_____

_____

_____

_____

Self-Assessment Checklist	
I followed instructions to **make a model** of inheritance of flower color in plants.	_____
I made **observations** of the frequency of appearance of flower colors in a model of plant reproduction and inheritance.	_____
I determined how many red-flowered and white-flowered offspring are produced when one parent has two genes for red flowers and one parent is hybrid.	_____
I determined how many red-flowered and white-flowered offspring are produced when both parents are hybrid.	_____
I made **inferences** about dominant and recessive inherited traits.	_____

Notes for Home Your child **investigated** the frequency of inheritance of genes and traits by making a model.
Home Activity: Follow the same procedure to model the frequency of inheritance of your child's eye color, hair color, or height.

© Scott Foresman 5

Surveying Inherited Traits

State the Problem

Are some forms of inherited traits more common than others?

Formulate Your Hypothesis

Which form of each of the traits shown do you think is more common among students in your class? Write your **hypothesis.**

_____

_____

_____

_____

Identify and Control the Variables

Who you survey is a **variable** you can control. Use a sample of students, not just those who are your friends or who sit near you. Survey the same group of students for all the traits on your list. Try to survey at least 20 students.

Test Your Hypothesis

3. Record your data in the chart.

Collect Your Data

	Tally of students	Total
Can curl tongue		
Cannot curl tongue		
Unattached earlobe		
Attached earlobe		
Widow's peak		
No widow's peak		

© Scott Foresman 5

Interpret Your Data

Use the data from your chart to make a bar graph.

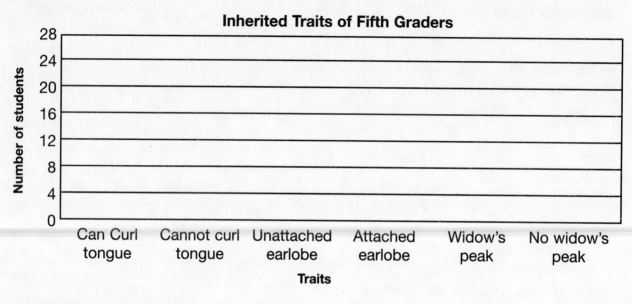

Inherited Traits of Fifth Graders

State Your Conclusion

How do your results compare with your hypothesis? **Communicate** your results. Explain how the occurrence of traits varies among the students you surveyed.

_____

_____

Inquire Further

If you surveyed a larger group of students, how would your results be affected? Develop a plan to answer this or other questions you may have.

_____

_____

Self-Assessment Checklist	
I made a **hypothesis** about forms of traits.	_____
I **identified** and **controlled variables.**	_____
I followed instructions to conduct a **survey** to test my hypothesis.	_____
I **collected** and **interpreted data** by making a chart of my **observations** and making and studying a graph.	_____
I **communicated** by stating my conclusions.	_____

Notes for Home Your child **experimented** to see if some inherited traits are more common among students. *Home Activity:* Help your child survey family members and friends for the same traits; compare the results with those of the classroom experiment.

© Scott Foresman 5

Name _____ Date _____

Exploring Protective Coloring

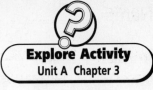

Explore

3. Which will be picked up more often, the newspaper or the construction paper moths? Why? Record your **prediction** and explanation.

_____

_____

_____

_____

_____

5. Count and record the number of each type of moth your team picked up.

_____

_____

Reflect

1. Was your prediction correct? Which type of moth was picked up more often?

_____

_____

_____

_____

2. Make an **inference** to answer the following question: Which moth would be more likely to survive in the newspaper habitat? Explain.

_____

_____

_____

_____

© Scott Foresman 5

Name _____ Date _____

Inquire Further

What would happen if the habitat was black? Develop a plan to answer this or other questions you may have.

_____

_____

_____

_____

_____

_____

_____

_____

_____

Self-Assessment Checklist	
I followed instructions to construct a moth habitat model.	_____
I **observed** the moths and recorded my **predictions** about which type of moth would be picked up more often.	_____
I recorded the number of each type of moth my team picked up.	_____
I determined which type of moth was picked up more often.	_____
I made an **inference** about protective coloration in moths.	_____

Notes for Home Your child explored how a moth's coloring protects it from being seen in its habitat.
Home Activity: Ask your child to name other animals whose coloring protects them from predators by helping them blend into their habitat.

© Scott Foresman 5

Name _____ Date _____

Investigating Eggshells

Follow This Procedure

4, 6, and 7. Record your **observations** in the chart.

	Observations
Number of books to break eggshells	
Eggshells in vinegar after five minutes	
Eggshells in vinegar overnight	

Interpret Your Results

1. Do you think a chicken egg is fragile or strong? Explain.

_____

_____

_____

2. Make an **inference** to answer the following question: How does the shell of an egg help a developing chick to survive in its habitat?

_____

_____

_____

_____

© Scott Foresman 5

3. How does vinegar affect the calcium compound?

_____

_____

_____

_____

Inquire Further

Does the size of the eggshell affect its strength? Develop a plan to answer this or other questions you may have.

_____

_____

_____

_____

_____

_____

_____

Self-Assessment Checklist	
I followed instructions to test the strength of eggshells.	___
I recorded my **observations** of the strength of eggshells.	___
I observed eggshells in vinegar and recorded my observations.	___
I explained how an eggshell is fragile or strong.	___
I made an **inference** about how the shell helps the developing chick survive in its habitat.	___

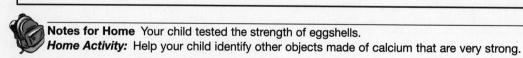

Notes for Home Your child tested the strength of eggshells.
Home Activity: Help your child identify other objects made of calcium that are very strong.

© Scott Foresman 5

Investigating Insulation

Follow This Procedure

6. Record your **prediction**, explanation, and **observations** in the chart.

	Shortening	No shortening
Prediction		
Start		
30 seconds		
1 minute		

Interpret Your Results

1. Compare your prediction with your results.

_____

2. Do you think that shortening is a good or a poor insulator? Explain.

_____

_____

_____

_____

3. Why is the fatty layer on an Arctic animal important? Compare it to your model.

_____

_____

_____

_____

© Scott Foresman 5

Inquire Further

What other materials can work as heat insulators? Develop a plan to answer this or other questions you may have.

_____

_____

_____

_____

_____

_____

_____

Self-Assessment Checklist

I followed instructions to **make** and **use** a **model** of fat insulation.	_____
I recorded my **prediction** and **observations**.	_____
I compared my prediction with my results.	_____
I explained why I thought shortening is a good or poor insulator.	_____
I explained why fat is important to Arctic animals.	_____

 Notes for Home Your child investigated how Arctic animals stay warm by making a model of fat insulation.
Home Activity: Help your child identify other animals that have a fatty layer to keep them warm.

© Scott Foresman 5

Exploring Parts of Soil

Explore

3. Describe three items in each group. Are there many like it, a few, or only one? Write a one-sentence summary of each group.

_____

_____

_____

_____

_____

_____

Reflect

1. How did you classify items as living, once-living, or nonliving?

_____

_____

_____

_____

2. Describe the appearance of the nonliving parts of the soil.

_____

_____

_____

© Scott Foresman 5

Inquire Further

If your soil was returned to the ground, what would happen to the once-living items over time? Develop a plan to answer this or other questions you may have.

_____

_____

_____

_____

_____

_____

_____

_____

Self-Assessment Checklist

I followed instructions to **observe** soil samples.	_____
I recorded my descriptions.	_____
I **communicated** by writing a one-sentence summary about each group I observed.	_____
I **classified** the contents of my soil sample as living, once-living, or nonliving.	_____
I described the appearance of the nonliving parts of the soil.	_____

Notes for Home Your child explored different materials found in soil.
Home Activity: Gather a handful of soil and ask your child to describe and classify the different materials for you.

© Scott Foresman 5

Name _____ Date _____

Investigating Owl Pellets

Follow This Procedure

2–7. Record your **observations** in the chart.

	Observations
Outside of pellet	
Inside of pellet	
Teeth	
Skulls	

Interpret Your Results

1. Make an **inference.** What does the presence of fur and feathers tell you about the owl's niche in the ecosystem?

   _____

   _____

   _____

2. Make an **inference.** Based on your observations of skulls and bones, does the owl eat mostly one species of prey or several different species? Explain.

   _____

   _____

   _____

© Scott Foresman 5

3. Think about the types of teeth you found. Make an inference. What type or types of food are eaten by the owl's prey?

_____

_____

_____

_____

_____

Inquire Further

How can you identify the species that the owl eats? Develop a plan to answer this or other questions you may have.

_____

_____

_____

_____

_____

_____

_____

_____

_____

Self-Assessment Checklist	
I followed instructions to examine an owl pellet.	_____
I recorded my **observations** of the owl pellet and its contents.	_____
I made an **inference** about the owl's niche in its ecosystem.	_____
I made an **inference** about the food the owl eats.	_____
I made an **inference** about the food eaten by the owl's prey.	_____

Notes for Home Your child learned about an owl's niche in its ecosystem by studying owl pellets.
Home Activity: Use an encyclopedia or other reference book to investigate the type of teeth a mouse has and speculate about what a mouse might eat.

© Scott Foresman 5

Name _____ Date _____

Experimenting with Carbon Dioxide and Photosynthesis

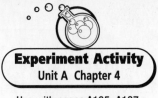

State the Problem

When a plant carries out photosynthesis it uses carbon dioxide. How does light affect the ability of a plant to use carbon dioxide?

Formulate Your Hypothesis

Will a plant exposed to light use more, less, or the same amount of carbon dioxide than a plant in the dark? Write your **hypothesis.**

_____

_____

_____

Identify and Control the Variables

The amount of light that the plants receive is the **variable** you can change. Keep the amount of bromothymol blue (BTB) solution, the length of the elodea, and the temperature the same.

Test Your Hypothesis

3.   What happens when a person exhales through a straw into the BTB solution?

_____

_____

5, 7–8.   Record your predictions and observations in the chart.

Collect Your Data

Cup	Color at start	Predictions	Color after 30 minutes
A			
B			
C			
D			

© Scott Foresman 5

Name _____ Date _____

Interpret Your Data

1. Which cup or cups still contained large amounts of carbon dioxide after 30 minutes?

_____

2. Which cup or cups showed evidence that carbon dioxide had been used after 30 minutes?

_____

State Your Conclusion

How do your results compare with your hypothesis? Write what you conclude about how the presence or absence of light affects a plant's ability to use carbon dioxide.

_____

_____

_____

Inquire Further

What would happen if you allowed the cups to remain open for several hours or overnight? Develop a plan to answer this or other questions you may have.

_____

_____

_____

Self-Assessment Checklist	
I made a **hypothesis** about how light affects the ability of a plant to use carbon dioxide.	_____
I **identified** and **controlled variables.**	_____
I followed instructions to perform an **experiment** using bromothymol blue to detect carbon dioxide in the cups.	_____
I **collected** and **interpreted data** by recording **predictions** and **observations** and by studying a chart.	_____
I **communicated** by stating my conclusion about how light affects a plant's ability to use carbon dioxide.	_____

 Notes for Home Your child **experimented** to see how light affects the ability of a plant to use carbon dioxide.
Home Activity: Help your child find out why a poinsettia plant needs to be in the dark for its leaves to turn red.

© Scott Foresman 5

Exploring Elements

Explore

2. Record your observations in the chart.

Object	Observations
Aluminum foil	
Penny	
Paper clip	
Graphite in a pencil	

3. Classify the objects into two groups and write the properties used to classify them beneath each group.

Group 1 **Properties**	**Group 2** **Properties**

Reflect

1. Which properties did you use to classify the objects?

_____

_____

_____

© Scott Foresman 5

2. Would you classify the elements oxygen and nitrogen in one of your groups or would you use another group to classify them? Explain.

_____

_____

_____

Inquire Further

What are some uses of the elements you observed? Develop a plan to answer this or other questions you may have.

_____

_____

_____

_____

Self-Assessment Checklist	
I followed instructions to **observe** objects made of one or more elements.	_____
I described each object and recorded my observations.	_____
I **classified** the objects by their properties.	_____
I listed the properties I used to classify the objects.	_____
I **communicated** by discussing how I classified elements with the class.	_____

 Notes for Home Your child observed and classified different materials.
Home Activity: Ask your child to classify different items in your home.

© Scott Foresman 5

Investigating Water

Follow This Procedure

7–8. Record your observations in the chart.

	Observations
Electric current flowing	
Electric current not flowing	

Interpret Your Results

1. What evidence do you have that during this activity water was separated into hydrogen and oxygen?

_____

_____

_____

_____

2. Make inferences to answer the following questions: At which pencil point was oxygen produced?

_____

_____

_____

At which pencil point was hydrogen produced? Explain.

_____

_____

_____

_____

© Scott Foresman 5

Inquire Further

Would the reaction work if you didn't add baking soda to the water? Develop a plan to answer this or other questions you may have.

_____

_____

_____

_____

_____

_____

_____

_____

Self-Assessment Checklist	
I followed instructions to separate water into the elements it is made of.	_____
I recorded my **observations** of the pencil tips as electric current flowed through water.	_____
I recorded my **observations** of the pencil tip as the electric current stopped flowing.	_____
I stated evidence that electric current can separate water into the elements it is made of.	_____
I made an **inference** about the elements produced at each pencil point.	_____

Notes for Home Your child split water into the elements it is made of—oxygen and hydrogen.
Home Activity: Ask your child how he or she knew at which pencil point hydrogen was produced and at which pencil point oxygen was produced.

© Scott Foresman 5

Name _____ Date _____

Investigating a Chemical Change

Follow This Procedure

5 and 6. Record your predictions and observations in the chart.

	Predictions	Observations
Baking soda and water		
Baking soda and vinegar		

Interpret Your Results

1. Make an inference to answer the following question: When you combined baking soda and water, was there evidence of a new substance being formed? Explain.

_____

_____

_____

_____

2. Make an inference to answer the following question: When you combined baking soda and vinegar, was there evidence of a new substance being formed? Explain.

_____

_____

_____

_____

© Scott Foresman 5

3. Which combination caused a chemical change to occur? Explain.

_____

_____

_____

_____

Inquire Further

What do you think would happen to the solutions if you allowed them to evaporate? Develop a plan to answer this or other questions you may have.

_____

_____

_____

_____

_____

_____

Self-Assessment Checklist	
I followed instructions to make a chemical change occur.	_____
I made **predictions** about what would happen when baking soda was added to water and to vinegar.	_____
I recorded my **observations.**	_____
I made **inferences** about new substances being formed.	_____
I **identified** the combination that caused a chemical change to occur.	_____

Notes for Home Your child produced and identified a physical and a chemical change.
Home Activity: Ask your child to name two physical changes and two chemical changes that occur at home.

© Scott Foresman 5

Exploring Motion

Explore

2. Observe the motion of the pendulum. When is it moving the slowest? the fastest?

_____

_____

_____

_____

3. How many swings does it take for the pendulum to knock down all the dominoes?

_____

_____

_____

_____

_____

Reflect

1. What did you do to control and change the pendulum's motion? How did you change the direction of the motion?

_____

_____

_____

_____

_____

© Scott Foresman 5

Inquire Further

What would happen to the pendulum's motion if you used a shorter string to make the pendulum? Develop a plan to answer this or other questions you may have.

_____

_____

_____

_____

_____

_____

_____

_____

_____

Self-Assessment Checklist	
I followed instructions to construct a pendulum.	_____
I **observed** the motion of the pendulum.	_____
I controlled and changed the pendulum's motion.	_____
I explained how I controlled and changed the motion of the pendulum.	_____
I **communicated** by discussing my observations of the pendulum's motion with the class.	_____

Notes for Home Your child built a pendulum and experimented with its motion.
Home Activity: Ask your child to build a simple pendulum and show one or two ways to change its motion.

© Scott Foresman 5

Name _____ Date _____

Investigating Force Used to Move Objects

Follow This Procedure

3–5. Record your observations in the chart.

Object	Length of stretched rubber band	
	Smooth surface	**Rough surface**
Empty box		

Interpret Your Results

1. How does the stretch of the rubber band change when you increase the mass of the object?

_____

_____

_____

Make an **inference** to answer the following question: How does the mass of an object affect the force needed to move the object?

_____

_____

_____

© Scott Foresman 5

2. How did your results change when you used a rough surface?

_____

_____

_____

Make an inference to answer the following question: How does the roughness of the surface affect the force needed to make objects move?

_____

_____

_____

Inquire Further

How could you reduce the force needed to move the objects? Develop a plan to answer this or other questions you may have.

_____

_____

_____

_____

Self-Assessment Checklist

I followed instructions to **measure** the length of a rubber band when moving objects of different masses.	_____
I recorded my **measurements** when moving objects across a smooth surface and a rough surface.	_____
I **compared** the amount of stretch needed to move objects of different masses.	_____
I **described** how my results changed when moving objects across a rough surface.	_____
I made **inferences** about the force needed to move objects of different masses across smooth and rough surfaces.	_____

 Notes for Home Your child measured the force needed to move objects of different masses across smooth and rough surfaces.
Home Activity: Ask your child to demonstrate that different amounts of force are needed to move an object across smooth and rough surfaces.

© Scott Foresman 5

Name _____ Date _____

Investigating Friction

Follow This Procedure

3–5. Record your observations and measurements.

Objects	Observations	Measurements
Eraser		
Stone		
Coin		
Button		
Toy car		

Interpret Your Results

1. Describe some properties of the objects that slide more easily.

_____

_____

_____

Describe some properties of the objects that slide less easily.

_____

_____

_____

_____

© Scott Foresman 5

2. Which object demonstrated the most friction with the board? Which demonstrated the least friction?

_____

_____

_____

Rank the objects according to how much friction was demonstrated, from most to least.

_____ _____ _____ _____ _____ _____

     most   least

Inquire Further

How could you reduce the friction with the board? Develop a plan to answer this or other questions you may have.

_____

_____

_____

_____

_____

Self-Assessment Checklist	
I followed instructions to demonstrate how friction affects different objects on a wooden ramp.	_____
I recorded my **observations** of the properties of the objects.	_____
I recorded my **measurements** of the board height needed to move each object.	_____
I described properties of objects that affect how the objects slid down a ramp.	_____
I **classified** by ranking the objects according to how much friction was demonstrated.	_____

 Notes for Home Your child **observed** and **measured** the height of a ramp necessary to overcome friction.
Home Activity: Ask your child to identify several objects in your home that would easily slide down a ramp.

© Scott Foresman 5

Name _____ Date _____

Experimenting with Balloon Rockets

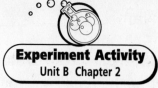
State the Problem

How does the size of a balloon opening affect how far a balloon rocket travels along a string?

Formulate Your Hypothesis

If you make the opening of a balloon smaller, will the distance the balloon rocket travels be reduced? Write your **hypothesis.**

_____

_____

_____

Identify and Control the Variables

The opening of the balloon is the **variable** you can change. The amount of air in each balloon and the size and shape of the balloon must remain the same. You must also release the balloon at the same point each time.

Test Your Hypothesis

1–8. Follow the steps on textbook pages B69–B70 to perform your experiment.

6–7. Record your data in the chart below.

Collect Your Data

Length of blown-up balloon: _____cm

Opening	Opening size	Distance balloon moves
Large	_____ mm	
Medium	_____ mm	
Small	_____ mm	

© Scott Foresman 5

Name _____ Date _____

Interpret Your Data

Use the data from your chart to make a bar graph.

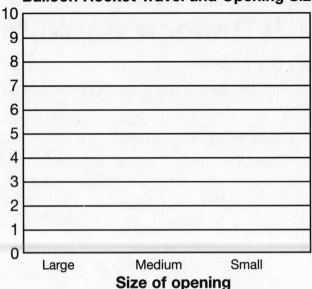

Balloon Rocket Travel and Opening Size

State Your Conclusion

How does your hypothesis compare with your results? Explain how the size of the opening affects the distance a balloon rocket can travel.

_____

_____

Inquire Further

How far would the balloon rockets travel if the string was held on an incline rather than horizontally? Develop a plan to answer this or other questions you may have.

_____

_____

Self-Assessment Checklist	
I made a **hypothesis** about the size of a balloon's opening and the distance it would travel.	_____
I **identified** and **controlled variables** and **experimented** to test my hypothesis.	_____
I **measured** different sizes of balloon openings and the distances the balloons travelled.	_____
I **collected** and **interpreted data** by making a chart and studying a graph.	_____
I **communicated** by stating my conclusion.	_____

© Scott Foresman 5

Notes for Home Your child **experimented** to determine how far a balloon rocket will travel.
Home Activity: Ask your child to explain which variables were controlled to complete the experiment.

Name _____ Date _____

Modeling Roller Coaster Motion

Explore

4. Make a drawing of the model. Mark on the drawing where you think the marble was speeding up and slowing down.

Reflect

1. What did you have to do to the posterboard to make the marble roll all the way over the hill?

_____

_____

_____

2. Make an **inference**. What do you think caused the changes in the marble's speed?

_____

_____

_____

© Scott Foresman 5

Inquire Further

Can you make the marble roll over two hills? Develop a plan to answer this or other questions you may have.

_____

_____

_____

_____

_____

_____

_____

_____

Self-Assessment Checklist

I followed instructions to make and use a **model** roller coaster.	_____
I **observed** the movement of the marble on the model roller coaster.	_____
I made a drawing of the model and marked where the marble sped up and slowed down.	_____
I described what I had to do to make the marble roll all the way over the hill.	_____
I made an inference about what caused changes in the marble's speed.	_____

Notes for Home Your child **made a model** of a roller coaster.
Home Activity: Ask your child to draw a simple roller coaster and explain how the height of the "hills" affects the coaster's ability to reach the end of the track.

© Scott Foresman 5

Name _____   Date _____

Investigating
Radiant Energy

Follow This Procedure

4–7. Use the chart to record your **observations.** Write an explanation for your
predictions.

_____

_____

_____

Appearance of paper	Predictions	Observations
Beneath construction paper		
Beneath wax paper		
Beneath plastic wrap		

Interpret Your Results

1. Which material blocked the most sunlight? Which blocked the least sunlight?

_____

_____

Explain why there was a difference.

_____

_____

_____

_____

© Scott Foresman 5

2. What evidence of an energy change did you observe in this activity?

_____

_____

_____

_____

Inquire Further

What other materials can be changed by radiant light energy? Develop a plan to answer this or other questions you may have.

_____

_____

_____

_____

_____

Self-Assessment Checklist

I followed instructions to test how radiant energy affects light-sensitive paper.	_____
I recorded my **predictions** and **observations.**	_____
I compared and contrasted the shapes produced on the light-sensitive paper.	_____
I stated which materials blocked the most and the least sunlight.	_____
I stated the evidence of an energy change I observed.	_____

Notes for Home Your child tested the ability of several materials to block radiant energy from the sun from reaching light-sensitive paper.
Home Activity: Ask your child to explain why some products such as vitamins or prescription medicines come in dark packages.

© Scott Foresman 5

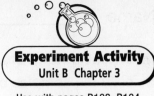

Experimenting with Sunscreens

State the Problem
Are there differences in the effectiveness of sunscreens?

Formulate Your Hypothesis
Do sunscreens with higher SPF values block sunlight better than sunscreens with lower SPF values? Write your **hypothesis.**

_____

_____

_____

Identify and Control the Variables
The SPF value of sunscreen is the **variable** you can change. Remember to keep all other variables—the amount of sunscreen and the length of time in the sun—the same for all the tests.

Test Your Hypothesis
Follow the steps on textbook pages B103–B104 to perform your **experiment.**

Collect Your Data.

Sample	SPF value	Sample of exposed paper	Rank (1 for most effective, to 3 for least effective)
1			
2			
3			
4	no SPF value		no sunscreen

© Scott Foresman 5

Interpret Your Data

Classify the samples by ranking them in order from most to least effective.

_____ _____ _____ _____

most effective   least effective

Describe the differences between the sunscreen paper samples and the control paper sample.

_____

_____

_____

State Your Conclusion

How do your results compare with your hypothesis?

_____

Were there great differences, little differences, or no differences among the sunscreen samples?

_____

Inquire Further

Does tanning lotion without sunscreen block sunlight? Develop a plan to answer this or other questions you may have.

_____

_____

Self-Assessment Checklist

I made a **hypothesis** about the effectiveness of sunscreens with different SPF values.

I **identified** and **controlled variables.**

I followed instructions to perform an **experiment.**

I **collected** and **interpreted** my **data** by **classifying** paper samples and ranking them from lightest to darkest.

I **communicated** by reporting my conclusion to the class.

_____

_____

_____

_____

_____

Notes for Home Your child **experimented** to find out if sunscreens with higher SPF values block more sunlight.
Home Activity: Ask your child to explain why one strip of transparent tape was tested without sunscreen.

© Scott Foresman 5

Exploring Electric Charges

Explore

3 and 4. Record your observations in the chart below.

Objects tested	Results	
	+ tape	**– tape**
Ruler rubbed with plastic wrap		
Comb rubbed with plastic wrap		
Ruler rubbed with wool cloth		
Comb rubbed with wool cloth		

Reflect

1. Which of the objects attracted the + tape? Which repelled the tape?

_____

_____

_____

Which of the objects attracted the – tape? Which repelled the tape?

_____

_____

_____

© Scott Foresman 5

2. Make an **inference.** Describe how charged objects act when brought near other charged objects.

_____

_____

_____

Inquire Further

Do objects without an electric charge attract the charged tape pieces? Develop a plan to answer this or other questions you may have.

_____

_____

_____

_____

Self-Assessment Checklist	
I followed instructions to make a charge tester.	_____
I tested objects rubbed with wool and recorded my **observations.**	_____
I tested objects rubbed with plastic wrap and recorded my observations.	_____
I listed objects that attracted and repelled the + tape and the – tape.	_____
I made an **inference** and described how charged objects act when brought near other charged objects.	_____

Notes for Home Your child made two charge testers and observed how the testers reacted when charged objects were brought near them.
Home Activity: Ask your child to explain what happened when charged objects were brought near the charge testers.

Name _____ Date _____

Testing Electrical Conductivity

Follow This Procedure

4–7. Record your observations in the chart.

Object	Prediction	Observation
Toothpick	X	
Penny	X	
Plastic coating on wire		
Stripped ends of wire		
Plastic straw		
Paper clip		
Rubber band		
Cardboard strip		
Aluminum foil strip		

Interpret Your Results

1. Classify each object as a conductor or insulator.

Conductors	Insulators

© Scott Foresman 5

What did the objects that were conductors have in common?

_____

What did the objects that were insulators have in common?

_____

2. Make an inference. Do you think a gold ring would conduct electricity? Would a piece of wood conduct electricity? Explain.

_____

_____

3. Make an inference. Why do you think the electrical cords in your home are covered with thick insulation?

_____

_____

_____

Inquire Further

What other objects conduct electricity? Can a liquid be a conductor? Develop a plan to answer these or other questions you may have.

_____

_____

_____

Self-Assessment Checklist	
I followed instructions and used the picture to build a circuit.	_____
I recorded my **predictions**, tested them with the circuit I built, and recorded my **observations.**	_____
I **classified** objects as conductors or insulators.	_____
I made an **inference** about objects that would or would not conduct electricity.	_____
I made an inference about insulation on electrical cords.	_____

Notes for Home Your child built a circuit and tested materials to see if they were electrical conductors or insulators.
Home Activity: Ask your child to identify two electrical conductors and two electrical insulators in your home. Have your child explain his or her choices.

© Scott Foresman 5

Making a Dimmer Switch

Follow This Procedure

3, 5. Draw the circuit.

6 and 7. Record your observations in the chart.

	Observation of bulb
As wire ends are moved apart	
As wire ends are moved closer together	

Interpret Your Results

1. Describe how the brightness of the bulb changed as you moved the wire ends apart and back together.

_____

_____

_____

_____

© Scott Foresman 5

2. On your drawing, write a B where the wire was placed when the light was brightest. Then write a D where the wire was placed when the light was dimmest.

3. Make an inference. Is graphite a perfect conductor, a perfect insulator, or something in between? Explain.

_____

_____

_____

_____

Inquire Further

What would happen if you used a bare copper wire instead of graphite to make a dimmer switch? Develop a plan to answer this or other questions you may have.

_____

_____

_____

_____

_____

_____

_____

Self-Assessment Checklist	
I followed instructions to make a dimmer switch.	_____
I recorded my **observations.**	_____
I described how the brightness of the bulb changed.	_____
I indicated on a drawing where the wire was placed when the bulb was brightest and dimmest.	_____
I made an **inference** about graphite as a conductor and insulator.	_____

Notes for Home Your child built a dimmer switch and made **inferences** about graphite as a conductor. **Home Activity:** Ask your child to explain how a dimmer switch works.

© Scott Foresman 5

Name _____ Date _____

Making a Current Detector

Follow This Procedure

5 and 6. Record your observations in the chart.

	Observations of current detector
Magnet moved inside of coil	
Current detector connected to battery	

Interpret Your Results

1. Why did the needle move when you moved the bar magnet back and forth in the wire coil?

_____

_____

_____

2. What can you **infer** about current produced by the moving magnet and the current produced by the battery?

_____

_____

_____

© Scott Foresman 5

Inquire Further

What are some ways you could increase the electric current produced by the moving magnet? Develop a plan to answer this or other questions you may have.

_____

_____

_____

_____

_____

Self-Assessment Checklist

I followed instructions to make a current detector.	_____
I **observed** the current detector when the magnet was moved inside the coil.	_____
I observed the current detector when it was connected to a battery.	_____
I recorded my observations.	_____
I made an **inference** about current produced by the moving magnet and the current produced by the battery.	_____

Notes for Home Your child built a current detector and used it to observe the effects of moving a magnet through a coil of wire.
Home Activity: Ask your child to make a model of the activity using a cardboard tube, string, and a drawing of a compass.

© Scott Foresman 5

Exploring a Model of the Earth's Layers

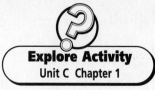

Reflect

1. Compare and contrast the different layers. What **observations** can you make about the layers?

_____

_____

_____

_____

_____

_____

_____

_____

_____

2. How do you think your model is different from the earth?

_____

_____

_____

_____

_____

_____

_____

_____

© Scott Foresman 5

Name _____ Date _____

Inquire Further

How could you change your model to show oceans and land masses of the earth?
Develop a plan to answer this or other questions you may have.

_____

_____

_____

_____

_____

_____

_____

Self-Assessment Checklist	
I followed instructions to make a **model** of the earth.	_____
I **measured** the layers of the model.	_____
I **recorded** observations about my model.	_____
I **compared** the layers of my model.	_____
I compared my model to the earth.	_____

Notes for Home Your child **explored a model** of the earth's layers.
Home Activity: Encourage your child to look for pictures of the earth's layers in magazines or travel brochures, or visit places in your community to see examples of these layers.

© Scott Foresman 5

Name _____ Date _____

Investigating Moving Continents

Follow This Procedure

1–4. Follow the steps on page C12 in your book.

Interpret Your Results

1. How well did your continents fit together? How did you decide to fit them together this way?

_____

_____

_____

_____

_____

_____

_____

_____

2. Record the differences and similarities between your map and the world map.

_____

_____

_____

_____

_____

_____

_____

_____

_____

© Scott Foresman 5

3. Do you see any patterns in the colored areas of your continents? If so, what are they?

_____

_____

_____

_____

_____

_____

Inquire Further

What other ways can the continents fit together? Develop a plan to answer this or other questions you may have.

_____

_____

_____

_____

_____

_____

Self-Assessment Checklist	
I followed instructions to **observe** the continent outlines and to **model** how continents may have fit together.	_____
I used different colors to shade in mountains, coal and glacier deposits, and fossils on each continent.	_____
I correctly labeled and cut out the continents, and fit them together.	_____
I **communicated** by discussing similarities and differences between my map and a world map.	_____
I described patterns on my map.	_____

Notes for Home Your child **investigated** how continents fit together.
Home Activity: Using a globe or a map of the world, have your child explain to you how the continents fit together like a puzzle and point out where some fossil and coal deposits are located.

© Scott Foresman 5

Investigating Weathering

Follow This Procedure

2–7. Record your **observations** in the chart.

	Observations
Broken chalk	
Chalk after shaking for 5 minutes with stones	
Chalk after placing in vinegar	
Chalk after removing from vinegar	

Interpret Your Results

1. Which cup or cups represented physical weathering? Which cup or cups represented chemical weathering?

_____

_____

_____

_____

_____

_____

© Scott Foresman 5

2. Was weathering more evident in one cup than the other? Compare and contrast the chalk in the cups.

_____

_____

_____

_____

_____

Inquire Further

How could you change the activity to investigate the combined effects of physical and chemical weathering? Develop a plan to answer this or other questions you may have.

_____

_____

_____

_____

_____

_____

Self-Assessment Checklist	
I followed instructions to **make a model** of weathering.	_____
I recorded my **observations** of the weathering of chalk by water and stones.	_____
I recorded my observations of the weathering of chalk by acid in vinegar.	_____
I identified the weathering of the chalk as physical or chemical weathering.	_____
I compared and contrasted the chalk in the different cups.	_____

Notes for Home Your child **investigated** the effects of physical and chemical weathering on chalk.
Home Activity: Look for signs of weathering on different objects outside (buildings, patio furniture, cars, flower pots, etc.).

© Scott Foresman 5

Name _____ Date _____

Experimenting with Crystal Formation

State the Problem
How does the rate of cooling affect crystal size?

Formulate Your Hypothesis
When cooling is faster will the size of alum crystals be larger, smaller, or will there be no effect?

_____

_____

Identify and Control the Variables
The rate of cooling the alum solution is the **variable** you can change. Keep the concentration of the solution and the amount of solution the same for each trial.

Test Your Hypothesis
1–9. Follow the steps on textbook pages C35–C36 to perform your experiment.

9. Record your data in the chart below.

Collect Your Data

Observations and measurements of crystals						
Cup	15 min.	30 min.	1 hour	2 hours	4 hours	Measurements
A						
B						
C						

Interpret Your Data
1. In which cup did crystals form the fastest? the slowest?

_____

© Scott Foresman 5

2. In which cup did the smallest crystals form? In which cup did the largest crystals form?

_____

3. Describe how the rate of cooling affects crystal size.

_____

_____

_____

State Your Conclusion

How did your results compare with your hypothesis? Write a summary of how the rate of cooling affects crystal size.

_____

_____

Inquire Further

What will happen if you keep the buttons in the solution until the solution evaporates? Develop a plan to answer this or other questions you may have.

_____

_____

_____

Self-Assessment Checklist

I made a **hypothesis** about the effect the rate of cooling has on the size of crystals that form.   _____

I **identified** and **controlled variables.**   _____

I followed instructions to perform an **experiment** to **observe** crystal formation.   _____

I **collected** and **interpreted data** by **recording observations** and by **measuring** and recording the size of the crystals.   _____

I **communicated** by stating my conclusion about the effect of the rate of cooling on crystal size.   _____

Notes for Home Your child **experimented** to see the effect the rate of cooling has on the size of crystals formed.
Home Activity: Ask your child to explain the results of the experiment to you.

© Scott Foresman 5

Exploring the Earth's Resources

Explore

2. Use the chart to write at least one way that each resource is used by people.

Resources	Uses of Resources

3. Use the chart to classify the objects into categories.

Resources that could be completely used up	
Resources which would be replenished within a human lifetime or less	
Resources which could never be used up	

© Scott Foresman 5

Name _____ Date _____

Reflect

1. How did you decide if a resource could be replenished?

_____

_____

_____

_____

2. Compare and contrast how different groups made their decisions.

_____

_____

_____

Inquire Further

Which resources in your classroom or home could be used up? Which could be replenished? Which could never be used up? Develop a plan to answer these or other questions you may have.

_____

_____

_____

_____

Self-Assessment Checklist	
I followed instructions to **observe** some of Earth's resources.	_____
I listed uses for the resources.	_____
I listed the resources that could be completely used up, the resources that could be replenished, and the resources that could never be used up.	_____
I recorded the objects that were classified in each group.	_____
I **communicated** by discussing if each resource could be replenished or not.	_____

 Notes for Home Your child **explored** Earth's resources.
Home Activity: Discuss with your child the steps your community has taken to protect Earth's resources.

© Scott Foresman 5

Lab Manual

Name _____   Date _____

Investigating
Water Pollution

Follow This Procedure
4–8. Record your observations in the chart.

	Observations
Level of lake water and water under hill	
Model before spraying	
Model after 15 minutes	
Model after 30 minutes	
Model after 1 hour	
Model after 2 hours	

Interpret Your Results

1. Describe how pollution on land can pollute underground and surface water.

_____

_____

_____

_____

_____

© Scott Foresman 5

2. Infer what might happen if water could flow down through a landfill into the ground below.

_____

_____

_____

3. Compare and contrast your model to a real lake and its surrounding land.

_____

_____

_____

Inquire Further

How difficult is it to clean the pollution from your model? Develop a plan to answer this or other questions you may have.

_____

_____

_____

_____

_____

Self-Assessment Checklist	
I followed instructions to **make** and **use** a **model** of underground water pollution.	_____
I recorded my **observations** about water pollution.	_____
I described how pollution on land can pollute underground and surface water.	_____
I **inferred** how landfills could contribute to water pollution.	_____
I compared and contrasted my model to a real lake and its surrounding land.	_____

© Scott Foresman 5

 Notes for Home Your child **investigated** how pollution on land can pollute underground and surface water.
Home Activity: Explain to your child where your household garbage goes and discuss the water sources that it could possibly pollute.

Investigating Air Pollution

Follow This Procedure

5–6. Record your **observations** and data in the chart.

Card Number	Location	Observations
1		
2		
3		
4		

Interpret Your Results

1. Compare and contrast your four cards. Describe the similarities and differences. Which location had the most particles? Which location had the fewest?

_____

_____

_____

_____

_____

2. Compare and contrast your cards with other groups. Did cards in similar locations show similar results?

_____

_____

_____

_____

3. Make an **inference.** Explain why there may be differences in the amount of pollution you observed in different locations.

_____

_____

_____

_____

_____

Inquire Further

What are some other ways to detect air pollution? Develop a plan to answer this or other questions you may have.

_____

_____

_____

_____

Self-Assessment Checklist	
I followed instructions to make an air pollution detector.	_____
I **observed** the particles on each card and recorded my observations.	_____
I compared and contrasted the cards.	_____
I **communicated** by comparing and contrasting my cards with those of other groups.	_____
I made an **inference** about pollution differences in different locations.	_____

Notes for Home Your child **made a model** air pollution detector to check pollution levels in different locations.
Home Activity: Ask your child to make predictions about the level of air pollution in different locations within your geographic area.

© Scott Foresman 5

Name _____ Date _____

Exploring How Sunlight Moves Water

Explore

5. Record your observations in the chart.

	Observations
Day 1 First observation	
Second observation	
Third observation	
Day 2 First observation	
Second observation	
Third observation	

Reflect

1. Draw some pictures of what you think happened in the pail. Draw a before-and-after picture.

© Scott Foresman 5

2. What role did the sunlight play in the pail setup?

_____

_____

_____

_____

Inquire Further

How could you make more water move into the cup in the same amount of time?
Develop a plan to answer this or other questions you may have.

_____

_____

_____

_____

_____

_____

Self-Assessment Checklist	
I followed instructions to make the setup.	_____
I **observed** the pail a few times a day for 1 or 2 days.	_____
I recorded my observations.	_____
I **communicated** by making drawings of what I think happened in the pail.	_____
I described the role of the sunlight in the setup.	_____

Notes for Home Your child **explored** how sunlight moves water through evaporation.
Home Activity: Ask your child to explain how puddles formed on cement when it rains dry up after the sun comes out.

© Scott Foresman 5

Name _____ Date _____

Investigating Sunlight and the Earth's Tilt

Follow this Procedure

6–7. Record your observations in the chart.

Tilt of the earth	Part of the Earth receiving more direct sunlight
One-quarter orbit (neither pole tilted toward sun)	
One-half orbit (South Pole tilted toward sun)	
Three-quarters orbit (neither pole tilted toward sun)	
Start/End of orbit (North Pole tilted toward sun)	

Interpret Your Results

1. Explain how the earth's tilt affects how directly light reaches different parts of the earth.

_____

_____

_____

_____

_____

_____

© Scott Foresman 5

Name _____ Date _____

2. Explain the difference in the seasons between the Northern and Southern Hemispheres.

_____

_____

_____

3. Make an inference to answer the question. Which position of the earth would be winter in the Northern Hemisphere? Explain.

_____

_____

_____

Inquire Further

How does the length of daylight time at the earth's poles change as the earth orbits the sun? Develop a plan to answer this or other questions you may have.

_____

_____

_____

_____

Self-Assessment Checklist	
I followed instructions to **model** the orbit of the earth.	_____
I **observed** the amount of light on the model.	_____
I recorded my observations.	_____
I explained how the earth's tilt affects how directly light reaches different parts of the earth.	_____
I made an **inference** about the position of the earth when it is winter in the Northern Hemisphere.	_____

Notes for Home Your child **modeled** how sunlight reaches different parts of the earth at different times of the year.
Home Activity: Looking at a globe or world map, discuss what the weather would be like in Australia or New Zealand in December and in June.

© Scott Foresman 5

Investigating How a Greenhouse Works

Follow This Procedure

5, 7. Record your measurements in the chart.

	Container without plastic wrap	Container with plastic wrap
Temperature at start		
Temperature at 10 minutes		
Temperature at 20 minutes		
Temperature at 30 minutes		

Interpret Your Results

1. How did the temperatures of the two containers compare before they were placed in sunlight?

_____

_____

_____

How did they compare after they were exposed to light for half an hour?

_____

_____

_____

2. Explain why it is important to use the same amount of soil in each container and to expose them to sunlight for the same amount of time.

_____

_____

_____

© Scott Foresman 5

3. Based on your measurements, which container do you think was like a greenhouse?

_____

_____

4. Explain how your model is similar to the greenhouse effect on the earth and how it is different.

_____

_____

_____

_____

Inquire Further

Would the results be different if you used water in the container instead of soil? Develop a plan to answer this or other questions you may have.

_____

_____

_____

_____

_____

_____

Self-Assessment Checklist	
I followed instructions to **make a model** of a greenhouse.	_____
I recorded my **measurements** of the temperatures of each container every ten minutes.	_____
I compared the air temperatures in the containers before and after they were exposed to sunlight.	_____
I **identified** and **controlled variables** in the activity and discussed why that is important.	_____
I compared my model to the greenhouse effect on the earth.	

Notes for Home Your child **made a model** of a greenhouse and investigated how it keeps plants warm. *Home Activity:* Ask your child to explain why it is dangerous to leave a pet in a car with the windows rolled up on a sunny day.

© Scott Foresman 5

Name _____ Date _____

Making a Model
of the Solar System

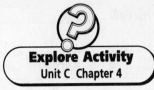

Reflect

Hold the Earth model next to the Venus model, then next to the Jupiter model.
Describe how the Earth compares in size to Venus and Jupiter.

_____

_____

_____

_____

_____

_____

_____

_____

Inquire Further

How many Earth models could be lined up along the diameter of the Jupiter model?
Develop a plan to answer this or other questions you may have.

_____

_____

_____

_____

_____

_____

_____

© Scott Foresman 5

Name _____ Date _____

Self-Assessment Checklist

I followed instructions to make **models** of the planets.

I used the chart to find the correct size for each planet model.

I **measured** each planet drawing to make sure it had the
proper diameter.

I **arranged** the planets in order of their position from the sun.

I described how the Earth compares in size to Venus and Jupiter.

_____

_____

_____

_____

_____

Notes for Home Your child **made a model** of the solar system.
Home Activity: With your child, make up a saying to help remember the order and names of the planets.

© Scott Foresman 5

Investigate Activity
Unit C Chapter 4

Use with pages C126–C127.

Making a Spectroscope

Follow This Procedure

5 and 6. Record your prediction and observations in the chart.

Prediction	Observations	Drawing

Interpret Your Results

1. Where have you seen a color pattern like the one in your drawing?

_____

_____

_____

_____

© Scott Foresman 5

Name _____ Date _____

2. Explain how the diffraction grating in the spectroscope changes the light from the light bulb.

_____

_____

_____

_____

_____

Inquire Further

What patterns do other sources of light produce when viewed with the spectroscope? Develop a plan to answer this or other questions you may have.

_____

_____

_____

_____

_____

Self-Assessment Checklist	
I followed instructions to make a spectroscope.	_____
I **predicted** how light would appear when looking through a spectroscope.	_____
I **observed** light from a bulb through the spectroscope.	_____
I recorded my prediction and observations, and made a drawing.	_____
I explained how the diffraction grating in a spectroscope changes the light from a light bulb.	_____

Notes for Home Your child **made a model** spectroscope to separate white light into the colors of the visible spectrum.
Home Activity: Ask your child to use information from this lesson to speculate about how a rainbow is formed.

© Scott Foresman 5

Investigating Lenses

Follow This Procedure

2–4 and **6.**   Record your observations in the chart.

	Observations
Description of lens shape	
Drawing of side view of lens	
Change caused by glass convex lens	
Change caused by smaller convex lens	
Appearance of object through telescope	

Interpret Your Results

1. Write an operational definition of a convex lens.

_____

_____

_____

_____

_____

2. Describe how to make and use a simple refracting telescope.

_____

_____

_____

_____

© Scott Foresman 5

Describe how to place the lenses and how to focus the telescope.

_____

_____

_____

_____

Describe how objects appear when viewed through the telescope.

_____

_____

_____

_____

Inquire Further

What happens if you use a concave lens as the eyepiece of a simple refracting telescope? Develop a plan to answer these or other questions you may have.

_____

_____

_____

_____

_____

Self-Assessment Checklist	
I followed instructions to record **observations** of objects through convex lenses.	_____
I drew a diagram of a convex lens.	_____
I followed instructions to make and use a simple refracting telescope.	_____
I wrote an **operational definition** of a convex lens.	_____
I described how to make and use a simple refracting telescope.	_____

 Notes for Home Your child **investigated** how convex lenses change the way objects appear.
Home Activity: Challenge your child to think of practical uses for convex lenses in everyday life.

© Scott Foresman 5

Name _____ Date _____

Exploring Lung Volume

Explore

3. **Measure** and record the diameter of the soap ring left on the bag.

_____

_____

Reflect

Make an **inference**. What might account for differences in lung volumes among students?

_____

_____

_____

_____

Inquire Further

Can regular exercise help you increase your lung volume? Develop a plan to answer this or other questions you may have.

_____

_____

_____

_____

© Scott Foresman 5

Self-Assessment Checklist

I followed instructions to form a bubble dome. _____

I **measured** the diameter of my bubble after it burst. _____

I recorded my measurements. _____

I used information in the table to determine my lung volume. _____

I **inferred** why there may be differences in lung volume
among students. _____

Notes for Home Your child **measured** his or her lung volume by blowing a soap bubble.
Home Activity: Discuss with your child why working to increase lung capacity might be beneficial to a person's health.

© Scott Foresman 5

Name _____ Date _____

Making a Breathing Model

Follow This Procedure

5–6. Record your predictions and observations in the chart.

	Predictions	Observations
Balloon pulled down		
Balloon pushed up		

Interpret Your Results

1. How well did your predictions match your observations?

_____

_____

_____

2. Compare and contrast the workings of your model with the actual process of breathing. What similarities and differences do you note?

_____

_____

_____

_____

_____

_____

_____

_____

© Scott Foresman 5

3. **Make an inference.** What might be the advantage of having an especially strong diaphragm?

_____

_____

_____

Inquire Further

What happens if there is an open hole in the cup? Develop a plan to answer this or other questions you may have.

_____

_____

_____

_____

_____

Self-Assessment Checklist

I followed instructions to **make a model** of the respiratory system.

I recorded my **predictions** and **observations** about the workings of the model.

I compared my predictions and observations.

I compared and contrasted the model with the actual process of breathing.

I made an **inference** about the advantage of having an especially strong diaphragm.

Notes for Home Your child made a **model** of the respiratory system to show how the diaphragm aids breathing.
Home Activity: Have your child explain what a diaphragm is and how it aids breathing.

© Scott Foresman 5

Name _____ Date _____

Experimenting with Exercise and Carbon Dioxide

State the Problem

How does the body's activity level affect the amount of carbon dioxide exhaled?

Formulate Your Hypothesis

If you increase your activity level, will the amount of carbon dioxide exhaled increase, decrease, or stay the same? Write your **hypothesis.**

_____

_____

Identify and Control the Variables

Your activity level is the **variable** you can change. Remember to use the same amount of bromothymol blue solution for each trial.

Test Your Hypothesis

1–6. Follow the steps on textbook pages D25–D26 to perform an experiment.

Collect Your Data

Trial	Activity level	Amount of time for color change
1	After resting	
2	After walking	
3	After running	

Interpret Your Data

1. Use the data from your chart to make a bar graph.

Changes in Bromothymol Blue

220
200
180
160
140
120
100
80
60
40
20
0

Time in seconds

Resting   Walking   Running

© Scott Foresman 5

2. Study your graph. Describe what happened to the amount of time it took for bromothymol blue to turn greenish yellow as the activity level increased.

_____

_____

_____

_____

State Your Conclusion

How do your results compare with your hypothesis? Communicate your results by writing a paragraph. State how exercise affects the amount of carbon dioxide exhaled.

_____

_____

_____

Inquire Further

Does the amount of carbon dioxide exhaled by people of different heights vary? Develop a plan to answer this or other questions you may have.

_____

_____

_____

_____

Self-Assessment Checklist	
I made a **hypothesis** about exercise and exhaling carbon dioxide.	_____
I **identified** and **controlled variables.**	
I followed instructions to perform an **experiment.**	_____
I **collected** and **interpreted** my **data** by **recording measurements** and making and studying a graph.	_____
I **communicated** by stating my conclusion.	_____

Notes for Home Your child conducted an **experiment** to see how the body's activity level affects the amount of carbon dioxide exhaled.
Home Activity: Ask your child why it is important to have plenty of fresh air available during physical activity.

© Scott Foresman 5

Name _____ Date _____

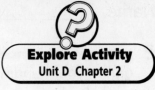

Exploring How Diseases Spread

Explore

4. Record your observations in the chart.

	Observations
Sheet 1	
Sheet 2	
Sheet 3	
Sheet 4	

Reflect

1. Describe how shaking hands can spread germs from person to person.

_____

_____

_____

_____

_____

© Scott Foresman 5

Name _____ Date _____

2. Make an **inference.** Besides shaking hands, what are some ways that germs can get on your hands?

_____

_____

_____

_____

Inquire Further

How can washing your hands affect the spread of germs? Develop a plan to answer this or other questions you may have.

_____

_____

_____

_____

_____

_____

Self-Assessment Checklist	
I followed instructions to model how some diseases can be spread.	_____
I **observed** handprints left on the four pieces of construction paper.	_____
I recorded my **observations.**	_____
I described how shaking hands can spread germs from person to person.	
I made an **inference** about ways that germs can get on hands.	_____

Notes for Home Your child **modeled** how some diseases can be spread from person to person by shaking hands.
Home Activity: Ask your child why it is important to wash hands with antibacterial soap.

© Scott Foresman 5

Investigate Activity
Unit D Chapter 2

Use with pages D56–D57.

Measuring Heart Rates

Follow This Procedure

3–4. Record your measurements in the chart.

Activity	Heartbeats in 10 seconds	Number of heartbeats per minute
Resting heart rate		
Exercising heart rate		

Interpret Your Results

1. Describe how your heart rate changed after exercise.

_____

_____

_____

_____

2. Make an **inference.** Why do you think your heart rate changed in this way?

_____

_____

_____

_____

_____

© Scott Foresman 5

3. What are some possible reasons for the variations in resting heart rates and exercising heart rates among your classmates?

_____

_____

_____

_____

_____

Inquire Further

If you continue doing jumping jacks, how will your heart rate change? Develop a plan to answer this or other questions you may have.

_____

_____

_____

_____

Self-Assessment Checklist	
I followed instructions to **measure** my resting heart rate and my exercising heart rate.	_____
I **collected data** by recording **measurements** in a chart.	_____
I described how my heart rate changed after exercise.	_____
I made an **inference** about why my heart rate changed when I exercised.	_____
I **communicated** by discussing possible reasons for variations in resting heart rates and exercising heart rates.	_____

Notes for Home Your child **measured** his or her resting heart rate and exercising heart rate.
Home Activity: Have your child show you how to find your resting heart rate and then compare his or her resting heart rate to yours.

© Scott Foresman 5

Contents   Part 2: Performance-Based Assessment

UNIT A   LIFE SCIENCE

Activity Preview: You will imagine that you and your partner have entered the local Science Fair. Your task is to place samples representing living and nonliving things on a poster along with samples of producers, consumers, and decomposers.

UNIT B   PHYSICAL SCIENCE

Activity Preview: You will imagine that you work in a science and energy museum. You have been asked to complete the information on the tags for an exhibit on potential and kinetic energy. The tags describe the types of energy in the exhibits.

UNIT C   EARTH SCIENCE

Activity Preview: You will imagine that you are an apprentice in an architecture office. The head architect asks you to select the best material to be used on the outside of a building for the entrance, front walkway, and front stairs.

UNIT D   THE HUMAN BODY

Activity Preview: You will imagine that you and your partner have delayed turning in your science lab reports until the last minute. Your partner has graphed the results, but her computer crashed before she could label the graphs. Now you have to accurately label the graphs.

© Scott Foresman 5

© Scott Foresman 5

Imagine that you and your partner have entered the local Science Fair. Your entry focuses on living and nonliving things. Your task is to place samples representing living and nonliving things on a poster. You must also place samples of producers, consumers, and decomposers. Make observations of samples A, B, C, D, E, and F and then decide which sample belongs where on the poster.

My Data Collection

Station 1

Use the card at the station to correctly set up the equipment.

Exhibit 1

Look at samples A and B closely. Use the hand lens alone or the hand lens and the microscope. Draw a sketch of what you observe. Label any of the following structures you see: *cell membrane, cell wall, nucleus, cytoplasm, vascular system, and chloroplast.*

Station 2

Use the card at the station to correctly set up the equipment.

Exhibit 2

Look at samples C and D closely. Use the hand lens alone or the hand lens and the microscope. Draw a sketch of what you observe. Label any of the following structures you see: *cell membrane, cell wall, nucleus, cytoplasm, vascular system, and chloroplast.*

© Scott Foresman 5

Station 3

Use the card at the station to correctly set up the equipment.

Exhibit 3

Look at samples C and D closely. Use the hand lens alone or the hand lens and the microscope. Draw a sketch of what you observe. Label any of the following structures you see: *cell membrane, cell wall, nucleus, cytoplasm, vascular system, and chloroplast.*

My Data Analysis

Now you have taken a close look at all the samples. Use your observations and what you know about living things to decide where to place each sample on the poster. Explain your choices.

	Exhibit 1 Producer	Exhibit 2 Consumer	Exhibit 3 Decomposer	Exhibit 4 Nonliving
Slide **Sample**				

_____

_____

_____

_____

_____

_____

© Scott Foresman 5

Imagine that you work in a science and energy museum. You've been asked to complete the information on the tags for an exhibit on potential and kinetic energy. The tags describe the types of energy in the exhibits.

My Data Collection

Station 1

Use the card at the station to correctly set up the equipment.

Exhibit 1

Turn on both flashlights. Observe what happens.

• Compare the energy changes, if any, you observe.

_____

_____

_____

_____

_____

_____

Station 2

Use the card at the station to correctly set up the equipment.

Exhibit 2

Shine the flashlight on the radiometer. Identify any type or kind of energy you observe. Describe how the speed of the vanes changes when the light is at different distances.

• Record your observations.

_____

_____

_____

_____

_____

_____

© Scott Foresman 5

Station 3

Use the card at the station to correctly set up the equipment.

Exhibit 3

Turn on both flashlights. Observe what happens. Use the materials on the table to show that one of the flashlights has more potential energy than the other.

- Describe how you were able to show that one flashlight had more potential energy and could do work.

_____

_____

_____

- Describe any observations you make about kinetic energy.

_____

_____

_____

My Data Analysis

Now that you have tested each part of the exhibit, use the data you have collected and what you know about energy to complete the following exhibit tags by filling in the blanks.

Exhibit 1 Tag

Flashlight _____ has more stored, or potential, energy. The flashlights have different amounts of potential energy because

_____.

Exhibit 2 Tag

The _____ energy from the flashlight did work by making the _____. The vanes turned _____ when the flashlight was close to the radiometer. The turning vanes are an example of _____ energy.

Exhibit 3 Tag

Flashlight _____ has more stored, or potential, energy. You can show that flashlight _____ has potential energy by showing that it can _____. Flashlight _____ has kinetic energy while _____.

© Scott Foresman 5

Name _____ Date _____

Suppose that you are an apprentice in an architecture office. The head architect asks you to select the best material for the outside of a new building. The material will be used for the entrance, front walkway, and front stairs of a public building. Consider the properties of samples A, B, C, and D as you make a recommendation for the material.

My Data Collection

Station 1

Use the card at the station to correctly set up the equipment.

Material Test 1

Look closely at the samples labeled A and B. Use the ruler and the hand lens to observe the samples and compare their color, luster, and breakage pattern.

• Record your observations.

_____

_____

_____

_____

_____

Station 2

Use the card at the station to correctly set up the equipment.

Material Test 1

Look closely at the samples labeled C and D. Use the ruler and the hand lens to observe the samples and compare their color, luster, and breakage pattern.

• Record your observations.

_____

_____

_____

_____

_____

© Scott Foresman 5

Station 3

Use the card at the station to correctly set up the equipment.

Exhibit 3

Decide which sample is made up of more than one mineral. Use your fingernail and a steel nail to test the hardness of samples that are made up of only one mineral.

Use your observations to complete the table. Answer *yes* or *no*.

	A	B	C	D
One mineral in the sample?				
Scratched by fingernail?				
Scratched by steel nail?				
Arrange the three single minerals from softest (1) to hardest (3).				

My Data Analysis

Now you have completed the materials tests. Use the data you've collected and what you know about rocks, minerals, and physical weathering to make a suggestion for materials to use in a building.

Select the sample you would suggest to use for the entrance way, front walkway, and stairs of a public building. Explain your choice.

_____

_____

_____

_____

© Scott Foresman 5

Imagine that you and your partner have delayed turning in your science lab reports until the last minute. Your partner has graphed the results, but her computer crashed before she could label the graphs. Use the results of the following activities to accurately label the graphs.

My Data Collection

Station 1

Use the card at the station to correctly set up the equipment.

Activity 1

Follow the directions in the illustration to take your pulse as you sit quietly at the lab table. Then jump rope for 25 rope turns and take your pulse a second time. Resume jumping rope, taking your pulse three more times— at 50, 75, and 100 rope turns.

- Record your observations.

_____

_____

_____

_____

_____

Station 2

Use the card at the station to correctly set up the equipment.

Activity 2

Squeeze the rubber ball as quickly as you can. Count the number of squeezes you can complete in 30 seconds. Continue squeezing the ball for two more minutes, counting the number of squeezes each 30 seconds.

- Record your observations.

_____

_____

_____

_____

_____

© Scott Foresman 5

Station 3

Use the card at the station to correctly set up the equipment.

Activity 3

Use the counters to make a model of the growth of a virus. Place one counter by itself. Then use counters to show how many cells exist after the first cell divides in two. Next show how many cells there are after each of those cells divides in two. Continue until you have modeled 5 cell divisions.

- Draw a picture of your model.

My Data Analysis

Now you have completed each of the activities. Use the data you've collected to correctly describe each of the following graphs.

Graph A

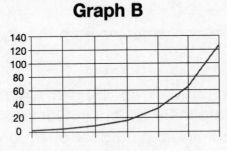

Graph B

Graph C

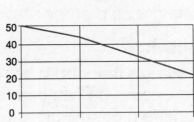

Explain your choices.

_____

_____

_____

_____

© Scott Foresman 5

Contents   Part 3: Science Process Skills

© Scott Foresman 5

© Scott Foresman 5

Name _____ Date _____

Practice Observing

Follow This Procedure

1–7. Record your observations and drawings in the chart.

	Observations of leaves on three trees	Other observations about the three trees	How many trees on the way to school?
Day 1			
Day 2			

Thinking About Your Thinking

Which observations did you most refine through repetition?

_____

_____

_____

_____

_____

_____

_____

© Scott Foresman 5

Compare notes with your classmates. Did they improve their observations by repeating them? Which ones did they most refine?

_____

_____

_____

_____

_____

_____

_____

_____

Self-Assessment Checklist	
I made careful **observations** using my senses.	_____
I recorded my observations.	_____
I refined my observations by observing the trees a second time.	_____

 Notes for Home Your child used several senses to observe trees.
Home Activity: Have your child make observations of a piece of furniture in your home. Then have your child repeat and refine those observations.

© Scott Foresman 5

Practice Communicating

Follow This Procedure

1–4. Record your descriptions of the rocks in the chart.

Rock	Description

How many types of rocks did you observe?

_____

Describe the rocks by their size, color, and hardness.

_____

_____

_____

5. Describe how the rocks vary. Describe similarities and differences.

_____

_____

_____

_____

© Scott Foresman 5

6. Make a chart of the qualities of your rocks.

Thinking About Your Thinking

Compare your chart to those of your classmates. How were they alike and different?

_____

_____

_____

How would the rocks be different in an environment unlike the one you live in? Why do you think this is so?

_____

_____

_____

Self-Assessment Checklist	
I **observed** rocks and described them by various qualities.	_____
I recorded my descriptions in a chart.	_____
I made a graph of the qualities listed in my chart.	_____
I **compared** my graph to those of my classmates.	_____

Notes for Home Your child observed rocks and wrote descriptions distinguishing one from another.
Home Activity: Have your child choose three pieces of furniture in your home and describe each by their various qualities, similarities, and differences.

© Scott Foresman 5

Name _____ Date _____

Practice Classifying

Follow This Procedure

1–5. Record your data in the chart.

Name	Quartz	Pyrite	Graphite
Color			
Streak			
Luster			
Hardness			

Thinking About Your Thinking

Do any of these minerals have the same characteristics?

_____

_____

_____

_____

_____

_____

_____

© Scott Foresman 5

What uses do you think these minerals might have? Use your classification chart to help you answer this question.

_____

_____

_____

_____

_____

_____

_____

_____

Self-Assessment Checklist	
I **classified** minerals according to several different characteristics.	_____
I used the information in my classification chart to determine how the minerals are alike and different.	_____
I made **inferences** about what uses the minerals might have.	_____

Notes for Home Your child classified minerals according to different characteristics to discover their similarities and differences.
Home Activity: Gather several different rocks and have your child classify them according to characteristics such as hardness, shape, color, smoothness, etc.

© Scott Foresman 5

Practice Estimating and Measuring

Follow This Procedure

1–5. Record your estimates and measurements in the chart.

Object	Estimate	Actual measurement

Thinking About Your Thinking

Suppose you wanted to estimate and measure the length of your school hallway. Would you use your fingernail and metric ruler as your measuring tools? Why or why not?

_____

_____

_____

_____

© Scott Foresman 5

Name _____ Date _____

What other measuring tools might be more accurate?

_____

_____

_____

_____

_____

Self-Assessment Checklist	
I **estimated** the length of several objects.	_____
I used a centimeter ruler to accurately measure the length of several objects.	_____
I recorded my estimates and measurements in a chart.	_____
I compared my measurements with my partner's measurements.	_____

 Notes for Home Your child estimated the length of several objects.
Home Activity: Choose items in your home and have your child estimate their length and determine which measuring tools should be used to make an accurate measurement.

© Scott Foresman 5

Name _____   Date _____

Practice Inferring

Follow This Procedure   Use with page 15.

5. Have you ever seen a rainbow? Did it seem similar to what you have just observed?

_____

_____

_____

_____

_____

6. Based on your current observation and past experience, what can you infer about sunlight? Is it made of only one color? Is it a mixture of colors?

_____

_____

_____

_____

_____

Thinking About Your Thinking

List the steps you used to make an inference about the color spectrum of sunlight.

_____

_____

_____

_____

_____

_____

© Scott Foresman 5

How did combining past experience with current observations help you draw the correct inference?

_____

_____

_____

_____

_____

_____

Self-Assessment Checklist	
I followed instructions to **observe** the colors made by sunlight reflecting off a mirror.	
I made **inferences** based on my observations.	_____
I listed the steps I used to make an **inference** about the color spectrum of sunlight.	_____

Notes for Home Your child made inferences about the color spectrum of sunlight.
Home Activity: Help your child make an inference about the role of rain in the appearance of a rainbow.

© Scott Foresman 5

Name _____ Date _____

Practice Predicting

Follow This Procedure

1–6. Record your predictions and data in the chart.

	Drops of water that fit on the head of the penny		Drops of water that fit on the tail of the penny	
	Prediction	Actual	Prediction	Actual
Trial 1				
Trial 2				

Thinking About Your Thinking

Did you make an accurate prediction at Step 3 of how many drops of water would fit on the penny?

_____

_____

How about after you made some observations?

_____

© Scott Foresman 5

Name _____ Date _____

How did additional information give you a better chance to make an accurate prediction?

_____

_____

_____

_____

Was your prediction for the tails side more accurate than the heads side? Why do you think so?

_____

_____

_____

_____

_____

Self-Assessment Checklist	
I made **predictions** and recorded my predictions in a chart.	_____
I practiced the investigation and then made new predictions.	_____
I recorded the actual measurements in a chart and compared them to my predictions.	_____

 Notes for Home Your child predicted how many drops of water would fit on a penny.
Home Activity: Have your child predict how many 1/4 cups of water are needed to fill a jar or bowl.

© Scott Foresman 5

Practice Making Operational Definitions

Follow This Procedure

2. Use the space below to draw an object that produces sound and diagram how the sound is produced.

3. Write an operational definition for the object. What does it do?

_____

_____

_____

_____

_____

_____

© Scott Foresman 5

Thinking About Your Thinking

Choose another object and repeat the activity. Compare and contrast the two sound-producing objects. How are they alike and different?

_____

_____

_____

_____

_____

_____

Self-Assessment Checklist

I drew pictures of two sound-producing objects and diagrammed how the sound is produced from each.	_____
I wrote an **operational definition** for each of the objects.	_____
I compared and contrasted the two sound-producing objects.	_____

 Notes for Home Your child wrote an operational definition of a sound-producing object.
Home Activity: Have your child explain the four basic steps in writing an operational definition.

© Scott Foresman 5

Practice Making and Using Models

Follow This Procedure

3–4. Record your observations in the chart.

	Description of what happens to the dots
Blowing the balloon up	
Letting the air out	

5. If this model shows how air particles move as air is heated and cooled, what do the dots represent?

_____

_____

_____

_____

6. What does the process of blowing up the balloon represent?

_____

_____

_____

_____

© Scott Foresman 5

7. What does the process of letting the air out of the balloon represent?

_____

_____

_____

_____

_____

_____

Thinking About Your Thinking

Explain how this balloon model acts like the particles in air being heated and cooled. Does air expand when it is heated or cooled?

_____

_____

_____

_____

Self-Assessment Checklist	
I **made a model** of how air particles move as air is heated and cooled.	_____
I recorded my **observations** of my model in action in a chart.	_____
I answered questions about what the different parts of my model represent.	_____

 Notes for Home Your child made a model showing how air particles move as air is heated and cooled. *Home Activity:* Help your child think of other situations where a model would be a useful tool for studying something.

© Scott Foresman 5

Name _____ Date _____

Practice Formulating Questions and Hypotheses

Follow This Procedure

2–3. Record your estimations in the chart.

Object Name	Drop Time	Properties

4. Write a hypothesis about the objects and their drop time.

_____

_____

_____

© Scott Foresman 5

7. Which properties contributed to a fast drop time?

_____

_____

_____

_____

_____

_____

Thinking About Your Thinking

Was your hypothesis correct? Why or why not?

_____

_____

_____

_____

Self-Assessment Checklist	
I **estimated** the longest to shortest drop times for six different objects.	_____
I wrote a **hypothesis** about the objects and their drop time.	_____
I conducted an **experiment** to test my hypothesis.	_____
I drew **conclusions** about which properties contributed to a fast drop time.	_____

Notes for Home Your child wrote a hypothesis about the drop times of different objects through a cylinder of water.
Home Activity: Have your child explain to you why it is important to the scientific process to formulate questions and hypotheses.

© Scott Foresman 5

Name _____ Date _____

Practice Collecting and Interpreting Data

Use with page 25.

Process Skill Activity

Follow This Procedure

2. Record your data in the chart.

	Hours indoors	Hours outdoors
Monday		
Tuesday		
Wednesday		
Thursday		
Friday		
Saturday		
Sunday		
Total		

3. Take the data from your table and reorganize it into a chart or graph. Use different colors for indoor and outdoor time.

Time Spent Indoors/Outdoors

© Scott Foresman 5

Hours: 24 22 20 18 16 14 12 10 8 6 4 2 0

In Out — Monday
In Out — Tuesday
In Out — Wednesday
In Out — Thursday
In Out — Friday
In Out — Saturday
In Out — Sunday

Day of week

4. Interpret the data in your chart or graph to answer the following questions:
Where do you spend the most amount of time, indoors or outdoors?

_____

_____

Do you and your classmates spend the same amount of time indoors during
weekdays and weekends?

_____

_____

Can you interpret how you usually spend your "Tuesdays" from just one day of
data?

_____

_____

Thinking About Your Thinking

Could you have made as accurate an interpretation of your data if you had only
collected data for one day?

_____

_____

Would your data and interpretations vary if you collected it in the summer or the
winter? on a holiday?

_____

_____

How can you adjust your data to account for these changes?

_____

_____

Self-Assessment Checklist	
I **collected data** on how much time I spend indoors and outdoors and recorded it in a table.	_____
I organized the data from my table into a chart or graph.	_____
I **interpreted** the **data** in my chart or graph to answer questions.	_____

Notes for Home Your child collected and interpreted data on how much time he or she spends indoors and outdoors.
Home Activity: Have your child explain to you how to collect data and organize it in a chart or graph.

© Scott Foresman 5

Practice Identifying and Controlling Variables

Process Skill Activity

Use with page 27.

Follow This Procedure

3–4. Record your data in the chart.

Amount of salt	Length of time for salt to dissolve
1 teaspoon	
2 teaspoons	
3 teaspoons	
4 teaspoons	
5 teaspoons	

Thinking About Your Thinking

Which variable did you change?

_____

_____

_____

What is being tested? (Hint: What did you time?)

_____

_____

_____

_____

© Scott Foresman 5

Name _____ Date _____

Which variables were kept constant?

_____

_____

_____

What did you find out about how the amount of salt affects the length of time it takes the salt to dissolve?

_____

_____

_____

_____

Self-Assessment Checklist	
I conducted an **investigation** to see how **controlling** one **variable** affects another variable.	_____
I recorded my measurements in a chart.	_____
I determined which variables were changed, which were kept constant, and which responded to the change.	_____

 Notes for Home Your child conducted an experiment to practice controlling and identifying variables.
Home Activity: Have your child explain to you what it means to control variables in an experiment.

© Scott Foresman 5

Practice Experimenting

Follow This Procedure

2. Write a hypothesis to state which rubber band you think will stretch the most when 500 grams of weight are added.

_____

_____

4. Record the results of your experiment in the chart.

Rubber band width	Length before weight	Length after weight	Difference

6. Graph the results listed in your chart.

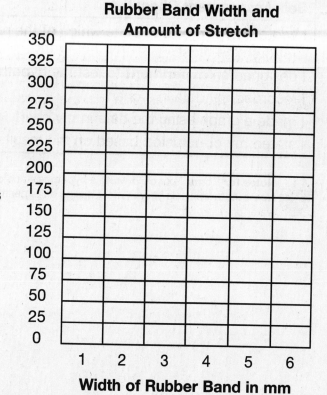

Rubber Band Width and Amount of Stretch

Stretch in millimeters

Width of Rubber Band in mm

7. State your conclusion.

_____

_____

_____

Thinking About Your Thinking

What did you learn from this investigation? How can having a too-specific hypothesis in the experimental process cause a problem? Can too broad a focus in later steps cause a problem as well? Explain.

_____

_____

_____

_____

_____

_____

Self-Assessment Checklist	
I wrote a **hypothesis** to state which of the rubber bands would stretch the most.	_____
I designed an **experiment** to test my hypothesis.	_____
I recorded my data in a chart.	_____
I made a graph using the data in my chart.	_____
I stated my **conclusion** based on the results of the experiment.	_____

 Notes for Home Your child wrote a hypothesis and designed an experiment to test it.
Home Activity: Help your student design an experiment to determine the affects of salt water on fresh water plant growth.

© Scott Foresman 5